BIGGEST NAMES IN SPORTS
RONALD ACUÑA JR.
by Hubert Walker

BASEBALL STAR

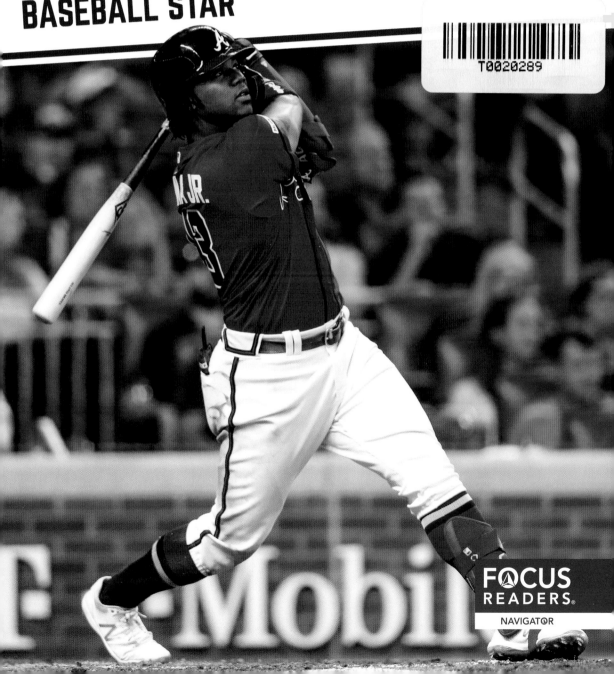

FOCUS READERS
NAVIGATOR

WWW.FOCUSREADERS.COM

Focus Readers is distributed by North Star Editions:
sales@northstareditions.com | 888-417-0195

Produced for Focus Readers by Red Line Editorial.

Photographs ©: John Bazemore/AP Images, cover, 1; David John Griffin/Icon Sportswire, 4–5; John Amis/AP Images, 7; Scott Winters/Icon Sportswire, 8–9; Gregory Bull/AP Images, 10; Tony Farlow/Four Seam Images/AP Images, 13; John Minchillo/AP Images, 14–15; Rich von Biberstein/Icon Sportswire, 17, 27; Brian Rothmuller/Icon Sportswire, 19; David Rosenblum/Icon Sportswire/AP Images, 20–21; Tony Tomsic/AP Images, 22; John Adams/Icon Sportswire/AP Images, 24; Red Line Editorial, 29

Library of Congress Cataloging-in-Publication Data
Names: Walker, Hubert, 1980- author.
Title: Ronald Acuña Jr. : baseball star / by Hubert Walker.
Description: Lake Elmo, MN : Focus Readers, 2021. | Series: Biggest names
  in sports | Includes index. | Audience: Grades 4-6
Identifiers: LCCN 2020033638 (print) | LCCN 2020033639 (ebook) | ISBN
  9781644936962 (hardcover) | ISBN 9781644937327 (paperback) | ISBN
  9781644938041 (pdf) | ISBN 9781644937686 (ebook)
Subjects: LCSH: Acuña, Ronald, Jr., 1997---Juvenile literature. | Baseball
  players--United States--Biography--Juvenile literature. | Baseball
  players--Venezuela--Biography--Juvenile literature.
Classification: LCC GV865.A264 W35 2021 (print) | LCC GV865.A264 (ebook)
  | DDC 796.357092 [B]--dc23
LC record available at https://lccn.loc.gov/2020033638
LC ebook record available at https://lccn.loc.gov/2020033639

Printed in the United States of America
Mankato, MN
012021

ABOUT THE AUTHOR

Hubert Walker enjoys running, hunting, and going to the dog park with his best pal. He grew up in Georgia but moved to Minnesota in 2018. Overall, he loves his new home, but he's not a fan of the cold winters.

TABLE OF CONTENTS

POSTSEASON GRAND SLAM

Ronald Acuña Jr. stepped up to the plate with the bases loaded. The **rookie** knew he had a chance to give the Atlanta Braves a huge lead. He was playing in Game 3 of the 2018 National League Division Series. Atlanta had two outs in the second inning. They led the Los Angeles Dodgers 1–0.

Ronald Acuña Jr. swings for the fences during Game 3 of the 2018 National League Division Series.

Acuña took three balls in a row. One more ball would result in a walk, and the runner on third would score. The Atlanta fans stood on their feet.

The pitcher threw a high fastball. Acuña thought it was another ball. So did everyone else in the stadium. But the umpire called it a strike.

The next pitch was right where Acuña wanted it. With a lightning-fast swing, he blasted the ball deep into center field. The ball soared over the fence, and the crowd roared. Acuña had just become the youngest player ever to hit a grand slam in the **postseason**. More importantly, he had given his team a 5–0 lead.

Acuña launches a grand slam during Game 3 of the 2018 National League Division Series.

Atlanta went on to win the game 6–5. Unfortunately for Atlanta fans, the Dodgers ended up winning the series. Even so, one thing was clear. Acuña was one of the hottest young stars in all of baseball.

BASEBALL FAMILY

Ronald Acuña Jr. was born on December 18, 1997. He grew up in the small town of La Sabana, Venezuela. Nearly everyone in town was crazy about baseball. And in Ronald Jr.'s family, baseball was serious business. Some of his family members had made it all the way to Major League Baseball (MLB).

Ronald Jr.'s cousin Alcides Escobar throws to first during a game with the Kansas City Royals.

In 2007, Ronald Jr.'s father played for Team Venezuela during the Pan American Games.

His father, Ronald Sr., spent several years in the minor leagues. However, Ronald Sr. never reached the majors. He admitted that he made poor choices during his career. For example, he didn't practice hard enough. He didn't **hustle**. Ronald Sr. told his son not to make the same mistakes.

Ronald Jr. took that lesson to heart. He put in hours and hours of practice. Over time, he developed into a great hitter with a strong arm. When he was 14 years old,

THE FAMILY BUSINESS

Ronald Acuña Jr. comes from a family of baseball players. His uncle José Escobar was the first one in the family to reach the majors. He played for the Cleveland Indians in 1991. Four of Acuña's cousins made it to the majors, too. Two of them, Kelvim Escobar and Alcides Escobar, spent more than a decade in MLB.

he told his father that he hoped to play baseball professionally.

There was just one problem. Most **scouts** thought he was too small. Few MLB teams even considered him. But a scout for the Atlanta Braves thought he saw potential in the skinny outfielder. Atlanta offered Ronald Jr. a **contract** in 2014. He was only 16 years old.

Ronald Jr. knew he wasn't ready for the majors yet. So, he started out in the minor leagues. In 2015, he moved to North Port, Florida. There, he played for the Gulf Coast League Braves. This team was at the lowest level of Atlanta's **farm system**.

Ronald Jr. slides headfirst into second during a minor league game in 2016.

Ronald Jr. impressed the coaches with his speed, arm strength, and hitting. Meanwhile, his body continued to develop. Ronald Jr. quickly moved up through the farm system. Soon, he was **dominating**. In 2017, he won the Minor League Player of the Year Award. A career in the majors was right around the corner.

ROOKIE OF THE YEAR

Ronald Acuña Jr. played his first major league game in April 2018. The rookie outfielder was only 20 years old. He was the youngest player in MLB.

In Acuña's first game, Atlanta faced the Cincinnati Reds. Acuña flied out in his first two at-bats. But in the eighth inning, he cracked a single up the middle. It was

Acuña waits for a pitch during his major league debut on April 25, 2018.

his first major league hit. The next batter lined a single to left field. Acuña sprinted toward second base. Most runners would have stopped there. But Acuña showed off his blazing speed. He rounded second and slid headfirst into third base.

Later in the inning, Atlanta batter Kurt Suzuki hit a single to center field. Acuña easily trotted home to score the first run of his career. It was a memorable night for Acuña. His run helped Atlanta beat Cincinnati 5–4.

At the beginning of the 2018 season, few people expected Atlanta to perform well. But the team surprised everyone. Acuña and second-year player Ozzie

Acuña completes a headfirst slide to steal second base during a 2018 game against the Colorado Rockies.

Albies often came up big in the **clutch**. The two players were best friends on the team. Albies and Acuña had played together in the minor leagues.

By the season's halfway point, Atlanta owned one of the best records in the National League. And the team never looked back. In August, Acuña homered in five straight games. He was the youngest player to do that in more than 100 years.

Atlanta easily won its division. But the team fell to the Dodgers during the postseason. Still, the baseball world had

LEADOFF MAN

In the second half of the 2018 season, Acuña became Atlanta's leadoff hitter. The leadoff hitter bats first in the lineup. He plays an important role. His job is to reach base so that the next batters can help him score. Acuña did exactly that. He racked up 127 hits and 78 runs during his rookie season. He also cranked out eight leadoff home runs. That was the most in team history.

Acuña grins after scoring a run during a September 2018 game against the San Francisco Giants.

taken notice of Acuña. After the season ended, the young outfielder was named National League Rookie of the Year.

FIVE-TOOL PLAYER

As a rookie, Ronald Acuña Jr. had proved how important he was to his team. Early in the 2019 season, the Braves showed their appreciation. They gave Acuña an eight-year, $100 million contract. The team's fans were thrilled that Acuña would be wearing an Atlanta uniform for many years to come.

Acuña signs autographs for fans during a 2019 spring training game.

Ken Griffey Jr. played a total of 22 seasons in MLB, mostly for the Seattle Mariners.

Acuña had been great as a rookie. But he was even better in his second year. Baseball experts started comparing Acuña to Ken Griffey Jr. That was high praise indeed. Most people agree that

Griffey was the best baseball player of the 1990s.

Similar to Griffey, Acuña is a five-tool player. That means he is good at all five of the skills that are needed in baseball. Many players have three or four of these tools. But it's rare for a player to have all five.

The first tool is speed. Acuña is one of the fastest base runners in the game. In 2019, he led the National League with 37 stolen bases.

The second tool is power. Acuña showed off his power by belting 41 home runs in 2019. Only four players in the league hit more.

Acuña belts a homer during a 2019 game against the Washington Nationals.

The third tool is hitting for average. Acuña hit an impressive .293 as a rookie. He followed that up by hitting .280 in his second year. In both seasons, he was one of the top hitters on his team. He also won the Silver Slugger Award in 2019.

This award goes to the league's best hitter at each position.

The fourth tool is fielding, and the fifth is arm strength. These defensive skills sometimes get less attention than the others. But Acuña always hustles

ROCKET ARM

Acuña's arm strength was on full display in a 2019 game against the Toronto Blue Jays. In the eighth inning, a Blue Jays batter ripped the ball to right field. The ball bounced against the fence as the batter rounded first base. Acuña fielded the ball and threw a laser to second. His throw was right on target. The shortstop caught the ball and easily tagged out the runner. It was the second time Acuña had thrown out a runner that night.

in the outfield. He impresses fans with his diving and leaping catches. And he frustrates many opposing teams by throwing out runners who try to take an extra base.

As a five-tool player, Acuña had a fundamental role in his team's success in 2019. For the second year in a row, the Braves won their division. However, they fell to the St. Louis Cardinals in the postseason.

In 2020, Atlanta won the division yet again. This time, Acuña helped his team make it all the way to the National League Championship Series. Atlanta won the first two games. But the Los Angeles

Acuña makes a spectacular leap to rob the Philadelphia Phillies of a home run during a 2019 game.

Dodgers came from behind and won the series in seven games.

It was a disappointing end to the season. But Atlanta fans felt excited about the future. With Acuña on the team, a World Series title seemed within reach.

RONALD ACUÑA JR.

- Height: 6 feet 0 inches (183 cm)
- Weight: 180 pounds (82 kg)
- Birth date: December 18, 1997
- Hometown: La Sabana, Venezuela
- Minor league teams: Danville Braves (2015); Gulf Coast League Braves (2015–2016); Rome Braves (2016); Florida Fire Frogs (2017); Mississippi Braves (2017); Gwinnett Stripers (2017–2018)
- MLB team: Atlanta Braves (2018–)
- Major awards: National League Rookie of the Year (2018); National League All-Star (2019); Silver Slugger Award (2019)

Danville

Rome

Gwinnett

Pearl

Atlanta

North Port

La Sabana

FOCUS ON
RONALD ACUÑA JR.

Write your answers on a separate piece of paper.

1. Write a sentence explaining the main idea of Chapter 2.

2. Which of the five tools do you think is most important? Why?

3. Which Atlanta teammate did Acuña play with in the minors?

> **A.** José Escobar
> **B.** Ken Griffey Jr.
> **C.** Ozzie Albies

4. What advantage did Ronald Jr. have when he was growing up in Venezuela?

> **A.** He had millions of dollars to spend on trainers.
> **B.** He came from a family of baseball players.
> **C.** He was bigger than the other players.

Answer key on page 32.

GLOSSARY

clutch
A difficult situation where the outcome of the game is in question.

contract
An agreement to pay someone a certain amount.

dominating
Showing that one player is clearly better than an opponent.

farm system
A group of minor league teams that help players develop their skills. Each MLB team has its own farm system. Good players usually move up to higher levels in the system.

hustle
To move quickly and give a full effort.

postseason
A set of games played after the regular season to decide which team will be the champion.

rookie
A professional athlete in his or her first year.

scouts
People who look for talented young players.

TO LEARN MORE

BOOKS

Braun, Eric. *Stathead Baseball: How Data Changed the Sport*. North Mankato, MN: Compass Point Books, 2019.

Chandler, Matt. *Pro Baseball Records: A Guide for Every Fan*. North Mankato, MN: Compass Point Books, 2019.

Frederick, Jace. *Baseball's New Wave: The Young Superstars Taking Over the Game*. Mendota Heights, MN: Press Room Editions, 2019.

NOTE TO EDUCATORS

Visit **www.focusreaders.com** to find lesson plans, activities, links, and other resources related to this title.

INDEX

Answer Key: **1.** Answers will vary; **2.** Answers will vary; **3.** C; **4.** B